RESCUE DOGS

Newfoundland and Saint Bernard dogs are used for rescue at sea, up mountains and in forests, as they are big and strong.

POLICE DOGS

German shepherds are the most common breed of police dog. They are very active, quick and protective, so they are ideal for this work. They are great at chasing and catching criminals, and have an excellent sense of smell, so they are good trackers. Human and dog police officers make an excellent team.

AIRPORT DOGS

Beagles in particular have a super sense of smell, and can sniff out illegal items being brought through airports. They save lives this way on a daily basis.

Dogs enjoy this kind of work because it exercises their brains and their sense of smell.

SLED DOGS

In cold countries, dogs are still used to pull sleds. Huskies are the best sled dogs, and were bred for this job.

DOG SPORTS

Dogs are involved in lots of sports. These are fun to be part of, but also fun to watch!

AGILITY COURSES

The dogs have to get around and through all sorts of obstacles as fast as possible, with their owners encouraging and prompting them. They run swiftly through tunnels, in and out between poles, over obstacles and up and down ramps. It's exciting to watch!

FLYBALL

Teams of dogs race each other, jumping over hurdles to reach a flyball box. When a dog presses a pedal on the box, a tennis ball flies up. The dog has to catch this and take it back to the handler. When the first dog gets back, the second dog is released and so on until all four dogs in the team have run. The first team with all dogs back successfully wins!

OBEDIENCE TRIALS

In these competitions, dogs and their owners show off the kinds of things you have learned in this book! The dogs must follow instructions precisely – sitting and staying, jumping and rolling over – and all with judges watching very closely.

These are just a few of many different dog sports. The world of dogs is huge, so make sure you research and find out as much as you can! A world of doggie fun awaits you.

CONTENTS

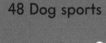

AUTHOR'S NOTE

From the beginning, dogs have been a big part of my life. My first dog was called Mars, and I was born at the same time as she had a litter of pups. All of the other pups went to new homes, and so Mars thought of me as her only remaining puppy, although she shared me with my parents. Mars would stand guard beside my buggy or sit beside my seat in the car. She didn't mind when I grabbed her ear or made loud noises.

I have had dogs all my life, of different shapes and sizes. They have been there with me in good times and bad times. This book is a collection of what I have learned from them, what they have learned from me and what others have taught us both.

Dogs are amazing friends. They care for you and look after you, without expecting more than a walk and a meal. They trust in humans, and we must earn the trust they give. If you give them care, they will give you love and loyalty.

INTRODUCTION

MAN'S BEST FRIEND

Dogs are the most popular pets in the world. The friendship between humans and dogs began over 15,000 years old, when dogs were wild wolves. This relationship helped both to survive, but dogs, like humans, are social creatures, so they found they were happy living with us.

Dogs are called 'man's best friend' for a reason. They have been great friends to humans for thousands of years.

ALL SHAPES AND SIZES

Nowadays, most dogs don't look like wolves. Over the years, they have gradually changed, adapting to the different jobs and purposes a dog can have.

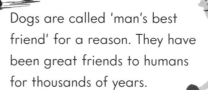

Dogs now come in all sorts of shapes and sizes, to suit their lifestyles and ours. Bigger, stronger dogs can be used on farms for herding cattle and sheep, and smaller dogs are used as watch dogs or companion dogs.

DOGS HEAL US!

The ancient Greeks believed that dogs had healing magic. They believed that while a sick person slept, the gods of health and healing would visit them in the form of a dog, licking them to heal their injuries and make them better. Today, dogs are still used to help people who are unwell. Therapy dogs can help people with high blood pressure or heart conditions just by sitting with them and being their lovable selves. Highly trained guide dogs also help people with impaired vision.

GREYFRIARS BOBBY

There are many examples throughout history of how amazingly loyal and brave dogs can be. One very loyal dog was Greyfriars Bobby, who lived in Scotland. When his owner died, Bobby stayed on his grave for fourteen years, until he himself died. A statue of Bobby still stands outside the Greyfriars cemetery.

HERO DOGS

Dogs have shown great courage in wars, helping to rescue people, carry messages and find important things. After the Second World War, the Dickin Medal was created for brave animals who served in the war. The medal has been awarded to pigeons and horses as well as dogs.

BEST FRIENDS

Dogs, like you, are curious and full of energy, and they love to explore. They are also very loving. Because we are so similar, people and dogs can form wonderful friendships. If you look after your dog well, have fun with them and keep them safe, you will become best friends.

Dogs are amazing creatures: they can run really fast; they can leap over fences or squeeze under them; they can catch a ball in their mouths midair. But there are a lot of things they can't do, so, like in any other friendship, it is important to be caring and to do whatever you can to help your friend.

TRUST, FUN AND KINDNESS

The key words for your friendship with your dog are trust, fun and kindness. We may be different animals, but humans and dogs both want to be treated well, so that should be your number one goal: to treat your dog well.

ARE YOU READY FOR A DOG?

A BIG DECISION

Getting a dog is a big decision. Before you and your family decide to get a dog, you should ask these questions:

- Do I have the time to care for him?
- Would everyone be happy to have a new member of the family?
- Am I willing to do everything I can to keep him happy and healthy?
- Can I be patient if he is bold?
- The biggest question of all is: Why do I want a dog?

WHY DO YOU WANT A DOG?

Do you just think a dog would be nice to cuddle and play with sometimes? Or are you really ready to care for a new friend, to take her for walks, to play with her and live with her all the time? Maybe you could write down the reasons why you would like a dog, and talk to your family about them.

A good dog owner is:
- *Patient*
- *Kind*
- *Clear when giving instructions*
- *Calm*
- *Understanding*
- *Positive*

CHOOSING YOUR DOG

HOW DO I CHOOSE?

Choosing a new dog is fun, but it is an important decision. You are choosing a new member of your family! There are lots of different types of dogs, of different sizes and with different amounts of energy. Here are some more questions to consider:

* What kind of personality would suit your family?
* What kind of life will your dog have?
* Is there much room for a dog in your home?
* Do you have a garden?
* How often do you and your family go for walks and exercise?

BREEDS

There are many different breeds of dog. With purebred dogs, because of the history of their breed, you can tell what kind of personality they will have, including their bad habits and their good qualities.

A mongrel is a mix of different breeds, while a crossbreed is a mix of two purebred dogs. Each mongrel and crossbreed is different from the next, and it may take time to see what their personality is like and also how big they will be. This can be fun to discover!

TO THE RESCUE!

You can get your dog from a licensed breeder, from friends or family whose dog has had puppies or from a rescue shelter. If you are thinking about a dog from a rescue shelter, ask the animal carers lots of questions: What is the dog's personality like? Where did he come from? What age is he? Find out as much as possible.

Dogs that have been brought to a rescue shelter may have been mistreated before. They may be nervous and need lots of love and care. You need to be extra patient with a rescue dog.

NAMING YOUR DOG

WHAT WILL WE CALL HER?

Choosing a name for your dog is really fun, but it will take a lot of time and discussion with your family. It must be a name that everyone likes and, most importantly, will use. Once you choose a name, you need to stick to it. One- and two-syllable names are easiest for dogs to learn. They quickly learn to recognise the rhythm of a two-syllable name in particular. Choose a name that rolls off your tongue and is easy to say quickly.

NAME TRAINING

When you begin training your dog, only use her name in a positive, happy way. Then she knows that when you say her name, something good will happen, like getting food, cuddles or walks.

During the first few days, when your dog is in another room, call her name happily and maybe clap your hands to encourage her to come and find you. Do this a few times a day. If your dog is on the other side of the room, crouch down to her level, open your arms wide and call her name. When she comes to you, give her lots of rubs and praise and even a treat if you have one. This will help your dog to recognise her name and also helps to teach her to come when called (which we will learn more about later).

Doggy sense: Never call your dog's name in anger, because he will be unlikely to respond — dogs are very sensitive to tone.

WELCOMING YOUR DOG INTO HIS NEW HOME

A WHOLE NEW WORLD

Imagine what it must be like for your new dog, being brought into your home. He was used to living somewhere else, and now he has been moved by strangers to this new place. It smells different, looks different and feels strange.

Try to take things slowly — stay with your dog as much as possible and help him explore this new world that he will soon love.

Your new dog needs:
- 🦴 *to feel safe*
- 🦴 *play and exercise*
- 🦴 *food and water*
- 🦴 *grooming*

NEW SCENTS, NEW SOUNDS

Your dog also needs to meet everyone who lives in your home, and get to know their scent. It is best if he meets people one at a time, so that he doesn't feel scared or overwhelmed.

It is a good idea to walk around your home with your dog when loud but normal noises are happening. Introduce your dog to the TV, the washing machine and the vacuum cleaner early on, so that he knows not to be afraid of these noisy things.

WHAT DO I NEED TO HAVE READY?

BED

It's best to make or buy a bed that will be big enough for your new dog when she is fully grown, and easily washable material is ideal.

COLLAR

Once you have a chosen a name for your dog, you can make or buy a name tag for her collar. It's a good idea to include a family phone number, in case she ever gets lost.

Top Tip: For the first few days, put a jumper that you wear a lot in your dog's bed so that she learns to associate your scent with comfort and safety.

LEAD

I recommend a thick rope lead with a padded handle. This means that your hand won't get too sore if your dog pulls a lot. You should always keep your dog close when walking near a busy road.

TOYS

It's a very good idea to have one or two toys for your dog, to prevent her from chewing other things — like shoes, socks, homework or furniture. Dogs, especially puppies, love to chew on things. Not only can they destroy valuable and important belongings, but they can choke or swallow things that may make them sick.

BOWLS

Your dog will need a water bowl and a food bowl. Stainless steel or ceramic bowls work best as your dog can't chew, carry or break them easily. Your dog should always have access to water.

KENNEL

A kennel is great to give your dog her own private place in the garden, but this is not a must-have.

HOUSE RULES

FAMILY MEETING!

Soon after your dog arrives, when you are getting to know him, you should sit down with your family to decide on some house rules.

Your rules might be things like:
- We never feed the dog from the table.
- The dog is not allowed on the couch.
- Every Saturday we will all go for a big walk together.
- We always feed the dog outside.
- We won't let the dog jump up on us.

These rules will be different for each family, and it's up to you to decide together what you think is fair for everyone, especially your new dog. Once the rules have been decided, it's a good idea to write them down and put the list on the fridge or somewhere that everyone will see.

STICK TO THE RULES

When you decide on your house rules, everyone needs to stick to them. If your dog is allowed to do something (like sit up on the couch) one day, and is not allowed to the next day, this will be confusing and upsetting for him.

Your dog relies on you and your family for all of his needs, so you should check he has everything he needs a few times a day. It could be useful to put this list on your fridge as well.

New Dog Check List:
- *Water*
- *Food*
- *Clean bed*
- *Has been spoken to and rubbed a few times an hour*
- *Has been outside to go to the toilet in the last hour*
- *Played some games*
- *Walk*
- *Training — ten minutes, a few times daily*

WALKING YOUR DOG

LET'S GO

Walking is important for your dog's body and mind. It's great for ours as well! Dogs who are exercised a lot are more relaxed and less likely to be nervous or hyper. It is good to walk your dog, whether he is large or small, twice a day. The length of the walks may vary from day to day, depending on you and your family's routine. It may also depend on your dog's size, age, breed and energy levels.

Some dogs are very energetic and need to be walked more regularly and for longer. If you don't have time some days to walk your dog twice, then be sure to play with her for twenty minutes, throwing a ball for her or playing some hide and seek games. This will help her to burn up energy, use her mind and bond with you. Just like us, dogs get bored, so you have to keep life as interesting as possible for them.

PUTTING ON THE LEAD

You should ask your dog to sit every time you attach her lead. Otherwise she will run, jump and roll around while you struggle to get the lead on her. She won't know that this is bad, because she will be rewarded straight away with a walk.

A DOGGIE-EYE VIEW

When walking your dog, try to imagine how she sees the world around her. To a dog who is not used to busy roads, cars and trucks seem like big roaring monsters! She will learn over time that she is safe with you on the lead, but you must be patient. If she is nervous, give her a rub, stop walking and distract her with a treat or by asking for the paw. Never ever give out to your dog for being nervous.

LOTS OF LEADS

Walking can be difficult if your dog pulls a lot on his collar. Some dogs may prefer a harness that wraps around their chest, which means that all of their strength is spread across their chest instead of just around their neck.

Another option is a nose halter, which is what I use for my dog, Rogue. This is like a collar, but with a small soft strap that goes loosely around Rogue's nose. This is very helpful, because Rogue likes to keep her nose to the ground, following smells. Without the nose halter, she would pull me through a hedge or over a wall in her search for the perfect smell.

You can try out different types of collars, harnesses and halters at your local pet shop.

PICK UP THE POO!

It is illegal to leave your dog's poo in public. You and your family should decide, before you get your dog, whose job it is to pick up the poo. Maybe this is something everyone in your family has to do, or maybe it's something only you or only an adult does. If you are the one who has to pick up the poo, you should remember to wash your hands as soon as you get home.

You can buy special poo bags in your local supermarket or you can use a pooper scooper, a handy gizmo specially designed for picking up dog poo.

TRAINING YOUR DOG

When your dog is learning new things, she needs plenty of time and repetition. Training uses a lot of your dog's brain energy, so it is best to keep training sessions short, and do them often – ten minutes around five times a day is ideal at the beginning. Learning is fun for your dog – they love to use their minds as much as possible.

REWARDS

When you are training your dog, you should reward the behaviours and actions that you like, and ignore or prevent the ones you don't like. Give her a treat or cuddles when she does the action you want. She will learn that if she does it again she will get a reward. Never punish your dog for not doing what you want her to do.

TO TRAIN YOUR DOG:

- 🐾 Make sure she is paying attention.
- 🐾 Say the command word (for example, 'sit').
- 🐾 Guide her, using hand movements, to do the action.
- 🐾 Praise her, rub her and/or give her a tasty treat.
- 🐾 Repeat all of this, at least twice more per session.

Doggie sense: Always be polite and kind to dogs. Never climb on them, jump on them or pull their fur or ears. Never do anything to a dog that you would not like done to you.

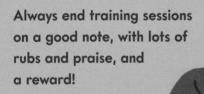

Always end training sessions on a good note, with lots of rubs and praise, and a reward!

Stop jumping

HELLO UP THERE!

Dogs jump up on people to get close to our faces and say hello. This can be cute when they are puppies, but when your dog gets bigger he could hurt you, and himself, by jumping up. You should gently get him out of this habit. This is something that could be in your house rules.

If, when your dog jumps up on you, you rub him and talk nicely to him, he will learn that jumping up on you is a good thing. So, to train him out of this habit you must do the opposite. Never invite or encourage your dog to jump up on you. If he does jump up, ignore him. Don't give out, but don't say anything, don't look at him and don't touch him. Turn away, fold your arms and ignore him until he stops.

HELLO DOWN THERE!

Once he gives up, crouch down so your faces are level with each other and give him lots of praise and rubs. If, when you stand up, he tries to jump up on you, ignore him again. Make sure your family do the same.

If you have visitors who are not used to dogs or are a bit nervous around dogs, put him on a lead and keep it on until he has calmed down.

DOG TRAINERS

If your dog is finding it hard to learn, you could get a qualified trainer to help. Puppy and dog training classes are held by many local dog charities, vets and other groups. You could also ask for information at your local pet shop.

TOILET TRAINING

WHERE DO I GO?

A very important lesson for your dog to learn is where to go to the toilet. She will need to go to the toilet a few times a day, whether she is a grown dog or a puppy.

Dogs are clean by nature. If you teach them that the whole house is their bed, they will want to go outside to go to the toilet.

Toilet training can be difficult, so you will need help. To toilet train your dog, you will need:

- 🐾 to be patient.
- 🐾 lots of newspaper or paper towels.
- 🐾 an adult to help you.

OOPS!

Don't expect your dog to learn overnight where she should go to the toilet.

Your new dog should sleep in a room in your home that has a wooden or tiled floor for the first few days. Untrained dogs (especially puppies) are used to going to the toilet whenever and wherever they want, so there will be a few accidents to begin with, and a tiled floor is easier to clean.

Never ever give out to your dog if she has an accident.

Going to the toilet is a natural thing, so she will not understand why you are annoyed.

LET'S GO OUT

Bring your new dog outside to go to the toilet regularly. In the first week or two, bring her out every hour during the day – straight after she eats, plays, exercises, wakes up, first thing in the morning and last thing at night. Like young human babies, puppies need to go to the toilet very often.

If you can stop her from going to the toilet indoors as much as possible, and praise her when she goes to the toilet outside, she will learn to associate going to the toilet with going outside.

SPOT THE SIGNS

If you see your dog going to the toilet in the house, bring her outside immediately. You will learn to spot the signals that she may need to go. She will pace the floor, get up after sleeping to sniff around, whine, bark or stand by the door. She may also hunt for somewhere out of sight to go to the toilet indoors, so keep an eye on her for the first few weeks.

Until your puppy is completely toilet trained, it's a good idea to put down newspaper in the places in the house where she will be for the first few weeks. This makes any accidents easier to clean up.

COMMANDS

SIT

This is the best place to start basic training, and it makes feeding and walking much easier.

1. Make sure you have your dog's attention.

2. Show him a treat in your hand — let him sniff it, or even lick it.

COME

Your dog should come when you call, whether at home or out in public. If he gets lost in a busy place, he needs to recognise this command from far away.

1. Ask an adult to hold your dog by his collar a few metres from you.

2. Show your dog a tasty treat (the smellier the better, so he can smell it from a distance).

3. Ask the adult to release the dog. Crouch down to his level, open your arms wide and call his name.

3. Raise the treat high above your dog's head, saying 'sit' loudly and clearly. Looking up at the treat will make him sit down.

4. As soon as he is sitting, give him the treat.

5. Repeat 5 times per training session.

4. When he reaches you, place one hand on his collar. Give him the treat, and lots of praise.

5. Repeat this regularly every day.

Call him sometimes just to give him a treat or a rub, then let him go back to playing. He will learn that good things happen when you call him.

DOWN

Only do this at home or where your dog feels safe, not in the park where another dog could suddenly approach.

1. Ask your dog to sit. Don't give him his treat yet.
2. Say 'down' or 'lie down', as you lower your hand slowly down to the ground and away from him. This guides him to lie down and creep forward a little.

It can take some time to learn, as he will expect a treat for sitting, but keep practising!

WAIT

This teaches your dog to wait while you pour out her dinner or open the door for her.

1. Ask your dog to sit, then hold out your palm flat facing him and say 'wait' or 'stay'.
2. With your hand up, count to three seconds. If she gets up or moves, start again.
3. Give her a treat if she stays still for a few seconds.
4. Keep practising over a few weeks, waiting longer before you give her the treat.
5. When she has learned to stay for ten seconds, begin moving away from her.
6. Start by taking one step back. If she moves, start again. Gradually move further and further away before asking her to come.

TRICKS

GIVE ME THE PAW

1. Ask your dog to sit.
2. Show him a tasty treat in your hand, and let him smell it through your closed fist.
3. Hold the closed fist in front of his chest and say 'give me the paw' or 'paw'.
4. Wait for him to lift his paw to get your attention or to nudge your fist.
5. When he lifts his paw off the ground even a little, say 'good boy' and give him the treat.
6. Try again, this time waiting for him to raise his paw further.
7. When he puts his paw on or near your hand, give him the treat and plenty of praise.
8. Repeat until your dog understands.

Doggie sense:
Don't try these tricks if your dog has a sore or injured paw.

HIGH FIVE

This is a fun extra bit to add to the 'give me the paw' command.

1. Ask your dog to sit.
2. Show him that you have a tasty treat in your hand.
3. Hold the closed fist in front of his chest.
4. Then, as he lifts his paw, raise your hand higher so that he has to reach higher to touch your fist.
5. Give him the treat once he touches your fist with his paw.
6. Each time you practise, raise your hand higher and higher, saying 'high five' as your hand softly touches his paw.
7. Give him lots of praise and rubs.
8. This trick is really fun, and great to show to friends and family.

GAMES

ON THE HUNT

Wolf pups play wrestling and hunting games as training for when they grow up and go hunting. Modern family dogs don't need to hunt, but they still play at hunting and fighting. They love to chase, freeze, creep up on things and then pounce on them.

HIDE AND SEEK

Hide and seek is great fun, and exercises your dog's sense of smell and her hunting skills.

- Ask your dog to sit, then let her sniff or see a piece of food.
- Ask her to 'wait' or 'stay', while you leave and hide the food in a different room.
- Let your dog into this room and ask her enthusiastically 'where is it?' or 'find it!' while she searches. When she is close, encourage her, saying 'good dog'.
- Once your dog understands the game, you can hide the food in harder hiding places.
- Give her praise and rubs as she eats the treat.

This is great fun, but try not to play it too often or your dog may lose interest. Instead of food, try hiding a member of your family!

Doggie sense: Don't play this game in the kitchen — it is not a good idea for your dog to get into the habit of searching for food there.

FETCH

This is by far the most popular game for dogs and their owners. It is great for giving your dog exercise when you're feeling lazy!

* Let your dog sniff a ball, stick or frisbee.
* Throw the object a short distance behind your dog, saying 'fetch'.
* Encourage your dog to follow you to the object and carry it back to where you threw it from. After a few tries, your dog will begin to understand that she is to 'fetch'.
* Reward your dog with lots of rubs and praise when she brings it back.

Some dogs don't like fetch, or find it boring. They may just want a chase, so they will get the ball but not bring it back!

CUPS

This game is great fun, and also exercises your dog's sense of smell.

* Set up three plastic cups upside down next to each other, either on the floor or out in the garden.
* Put a treat under one of them, then mix them around.
* Let your dog smell all the cups. As she stops at the cup with the prize, lift it up and let her have the treat.
* As she gets better at the game, she will find the treat faster. When this happens, add more cups.

TAKE A BREAK!

Dogs need plenty of rest just like us, so make sure to relax and take breaks when playing together. Always make sure there is water in your dog's bowl and that they can reach it. Make sure you drink some water too!

MEETING AND LIVING WITH OTHER DOGS AND ANIMALS

WHAT ARE YOU?

It is a good idea to begin to introduce your puppy or new dog to other dogs and animals at an early age, to get him used to them.

Always put your dog on the lead when going to see larger animals like cows, horses and bigger dogs. This means that you can control your dog and get him out of a scary situation quickly.

It is best to introduce your dog to other dogs that you know are well-behaved, so that your dog's first impressions of other dogs are good.

MEETING OTHER DOGS: THE SNIFF TEST

Dogs don't only sniff the ground; they also sniff other dogs' backsides and faces. This is a very important part of their communication with each other. By sniffing the ground, dogs can tell who has been there and whose territory they are in. However, sniffing another dog's backside tells your dog whether that dog is friendly or hostile, and male or female.

Dogs also sniff human backsides and pelvises in greeting. It works fine for dogs, but I would not recommend that you greet your family this way.

WHO'S THE BOSS?

If you already have other pets in your home, they need to be introduced to the new dog as quickly as possible.

Dogs who live in the same home can sometimes fight over space and ownership of the home. After some time, they usually come to an agreement – either one dog submits to the other, or they agree to share.

Bentley and Holly live in the same home and they agreed to share their home, but if there is ever a disagreement, Holly is the always the winner. Bentley is a gentle soul, who will submit to dogs that show any level of dominance.

All sorts of pets can live in harmony together in one home, but the bossiest animal will pretty much always be in charge.

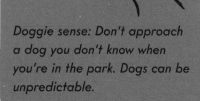

Doggie sense: Don't approach a dog you don't know when you're in the park. Dogs can be unpredictable.

If you have trouble getting your dog to get along with other pets in your home, it can help to bring your dog to training classes to get them used to being around other dogs.

FEEDING YOUR DOG

A BALANCED DIET

A healthy, balanced diet is vital for your dog's health and wellbeing. You need to make sure that she gets all the nutrients she needs to keep her fuelled for play, walks and general life. It is important that you don't feed your dog too much or too little.

ASK AN EXPERT

Your vet or local pet shop will help you choose the best dry food for your dog's breed, size and energy levels. Vets recommend feeding adult dogs twice daily, and puppies four times daily.

Dry food can help keep your dog's teeth clean and healthy. You can also add other things to dry food to keep it interesting. Healthy things that can be added to dry food include:

- green vegetables, for example broccoli, peas, carrots
- fish oils
- any oily fish

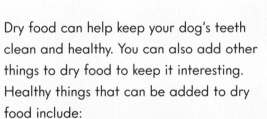

Doggie sense: Never give your dog a bone — it could splinter and hurt his mouth, throat and stomach.

WHERE'S MY DINNER?

Where and when you feed your dog is also very important. Dogs like routine, and it's best to have a set area or place where you always feed your dog, as well as a set time that you do it. Never feed him from the table, or he will begin to annoy you and your family while you eat.

It is best to feed your dog after you and your family have had your meal.

MMM, YUMMY!

Your dog's food may not look tasty to you, but it tastes great to them. You may think that eating the same thing every day must be boring, but in fact dogs taste food differently to us and have a much less developed sense of taste.

Did you know? We have nearly 9,000 taste buds in our mouths, while dogs have less than 2,000. Dogs are carnivores, mainly eating meat and fat, so they can taste a much more limited range of foods than us.

Bad foods

Dog's bodies look different to ours, and they also work differently. Some foods that we like, and that are good for us, are actually dangerous for dogs to eat. Here are some foods and drinks that you must never give to your dog:

Chocolate, coffee and caffeine

Grapes and raisins

Nuts

Salt and salty snack foods

Onions, garlic, chives

Milk and dairy

You may think you're being nice to your dog, giving her some of your food, but in fact any human processed food is bad for dogs.

LEADER OF THE PACK

Food is, of course, vital for your dog's survival. Her ancestors hunted for their own food, and brought back a meal for the pack. Now, your dog relies on you for food. Her instincts will tell her that you are the pack leader if you give her food and protection. To make sure that your dog listens to you, it can help if you are the family member that gives her her meals as much as possible.

Feeding time

We've already learned how to teach your dog to stay, but asking her to wait for her dinner can be a little bit trickier! You will need an adult to help with this.

- Put your dog on her lead and ask an adult to hold her.
- Pour out her dinner on a high table that she can't reach.
- Ask your dog to sit and stay.
- Place the bowl on the ground.
- If your dog tries to move forward, the adult should hold her back using the lead.
- When your dog sits back down and stays still, clap your hands twice while the adult releases their hold on the lead.
- Repeat this with the lead over a few days, until you think your dog understands.

With enough practice, you should then be able to pour your dog's food into her bowl on the floor, and she will wait until you clap, without the need for a lead. This makes feeding time a lot more relaxed and easy.

Doggie sense: Remember that your dog still has those primitive wolf instincts. Never move too close or touch her while she is eating.

GROOMING

Keeping your dog's coat clean and free of knots and tangles will help him look good and feel comfortable. There are many different coat types — long and short hair, curly and straight — and some require more care than others.

LOVELY MUD

Some dogs, like Bentley, like to jump into every muddy puddle they find. They have an instinct to camouflage themselves, to cover up their own scent.

Unfortunately, whatever dirt is on your dog will be spread all around your home and your car, and onto your hands, clothes and furniture. To clean your dog, let him dry and then brush the dried mud off his coat.

Only wash him if he has rolled in something smelly.

Did you know? Dogs' paws can be really smelly, but for a good reason — they have sweat glands are on the pads of their paws! Dogs also cool down by panting with their mouths wide open, letting the moisture in their mouths evaporate. It looks like they're laughing!

Bath time

Some dogs need to be washed more often than others. Ask your vet for advice. Lots of dogs love the bath, but some of them don't like it all. Some find water uncomfortable, or even scary, and will need a lot of reassurance at bath time.

WHAT DO I NEED?

You will need some equipment to give your dog a bath

- Some treats and toys to keep him busy while you wash and brush him
- A bath, whether your family bath or a portable dog bath (some very small dogs fit in the sink!)
- A large plastic cup or jug
- Gloves
- A spare collar and lead (that you don't mind getting wet)
- Shampoo: You can buy special dog shampoo that is gentle on their skin.
- A towel that is used only for your dog – an old towel will do.

Doggie sense: You will need an adult's help to wash your dog.

Rogue has a bath

There are different ways to wash your dog, or a dog groomer can wash her for you. This is how I wash Rogue. There is quite a lot of work involved in washing her, so I always get someone to hold and comfort her while I wash her.

- I fill the bath just up to the level of Rogue's ankles with warm water (not cold water – just like us, she doesn't like it).
- I use a large plastic jug to gently pour water on her coat, starting at the base of her neck and moving towards her tail, avoiding her face. I gently wipe her face with a wet cloth at the end.
- Then shampoo, and rinse.
- I give her lots of treats, pets and praise, so that she thinks of bath time as a pleasant experience.
- I use an old towel to dry her.

Top Tip: You should wear reusable rubber gloves when washing your dog. Your dog rolls in smelly stuff, so the gloves will protect your hands from any unwanted bacteria.

DO THE DOGGIE SHAKE

Now, be warned, once a dog is finished her bath and is free from your grasp, she will shake and shake and shake so that the water goes flying in all directions. It will go all over you and all over the room. Watching your dog shake is fun, but stand well back. She will shake her entire body, from her head to the end of her tail. It is very effective as well, and you will find that she dries very fast.

GROOMING

Red, who is a border terrier, is groomed professionally when his fur gets very long. His coat is sheared tight to the skin, his whole body is scrubbed and cleaned and the hair around his face is gently and carefully trimmed so he can see easier.

Other dogs, like Bentley, do not need professional grooming. His hair is long, but it stays the same length and never needs to be cut. Bentley sheds his hair naturally, leaving short blond hairs all over the car, the couch and his owner's clothes!

BRUSHING

It's a good idea to brush your dog gently every few days, and you should start when he is very young. Always give him a treat before and afterwards, so that he enjoys the experience. There are various different types of brushes and combs, which you can find at your local pet shop.

Some dogs don't like to be brushed and can try to wriggle away, so you will have to be patient. Many dogs love to be brushed and groomed, and many humans love brushing their dogs too!

COMMUNICATION, AFFECTION AND BONDING

WOLF PACK

Dogs may be pets now, but they still have some of the instincts of their ancestors. A very strong one is the pack instinct. This is why dogs like to be members of families – it reminds them of being wolves, although they don't know it!

COMMUNICATING WITH YOUR DOG

Dogs don't think the same way as we do. Their minds work very differently to ours, but this doesn't mean that we can't communicate with dogs. Learning how to communicate with your dog is the most important way to earn her respect and develop a happy, trusting relationship with her.

There are many talking dogs in movies and books. In the real world, however, dogs communicate mostly through actions and body language. All dogs are unique in how they act and communicate, but they share similar behaviours.

Doggie sense: Dogs can detect changes in our scent due to our emotions. This is how they know to comfort us when we're sad, to play with us when we are happy or to curl up beside us when we are tired. Dogs can become upset or worried because they know we are feeling that way. This is why it is good for your dog to have her own space where she can go and relax in peace.

A DOG'S WORLD

If you are having trouble understanding your dog, or she's having trouble understanding you, it can help to try to imagine the world through her eyes:

 What does she see when she looks at you?
 Do you look angry or friendly?
 Should she feel happy or scared?

LET ME OUT OF HERE!

Dogs can't speak to us in words, so they can find it difficult to tell us how they feel. This can lead to them feeling frustrated. Remember that if your dog acts angrily, it's probably because she is scared. If a dog feels trapped and in danger, she may bite as a way to get away from a scary situation. This usually only happens with strangers.

YOUR OWN LANGUAGE

You will learn to tell how your dog is feeling based on her face, posture or position, and the sounds she makes. As you get used to your dog, and she gets used to you, you will create your own unique ways of communicating.

Doggie sense: If your dog is often angry or aggressive, you should bring her to the vet. She may be sick, and feeling sensitive and scared. If her health is good but she is still behaving badly, you could take her to a trainer or behaviourist who could help her overcome her fears.

APPROACHING YOUR DOG

Be careful when you approach your dog to ensure that he feels comfortable and safe. Avoid sudden movements or loud noises near him, so that he doesn't become nervous when you approach. Your dog should always be happy when he sees you, and not worried that you will jump on him or shout at him.

- It is important that you don't do anything that could hurt your dog or make him uncomfortable.
- Be careful not to grab your dog's fur too tightly. You may be doing it to show you love him, but it can hurt.
- Get to know what your dog likes or dislikes. Most dogs find it relaxing to have the ends of their ears gently rubbed.
- Try to be aware of where your dog is in your home, so that you don't step on him or fall over him.

Doggie sense:
Never approach your dog
when they are
- *eating or having a treat*
- *playing with their favourite toy alone*
- *sleeping*
- *unwell or injured*

Doggie sense: Just like us, dogs like to have a break from everyone once in a while. Give your dog a cosy spot in the garden, or a corner of the house, that is his own little quiet place. If he goes there, leave him be – he'll come to you when he wants to play.

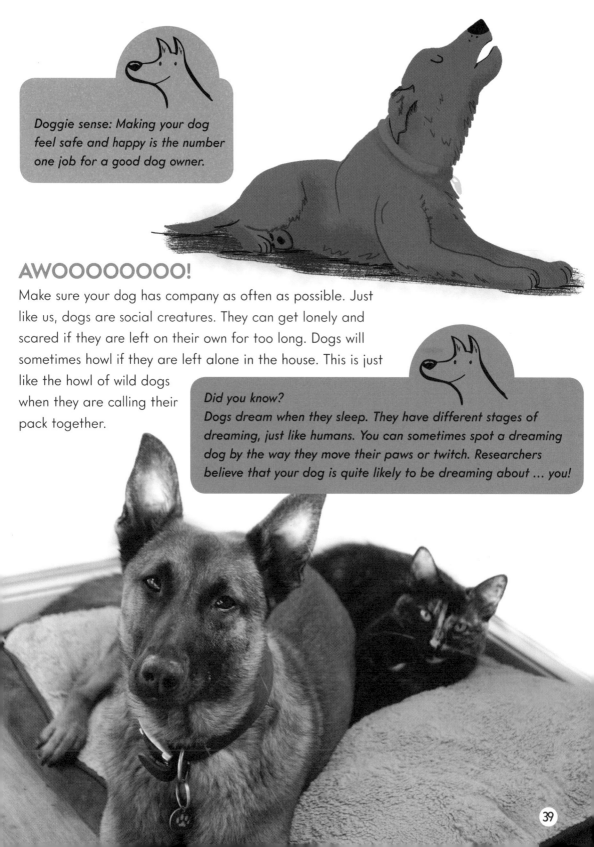

AWOOOOOOOO!

Make sure your dog has company as often as possible. Just like us, dogs are social creatures. They can get lonely and scared if they are left on their own for too long. Dogs will sometimes howl if they are left alone in the house. This is just like the howl of wild dogs when they are calling their pack together.

Did you know?
Dogs dream when they sleep. They have different stages of dreaming, just like humans. You can sometimes spot a dreaming dog by the way they move their paws or twitch. Researchers believe that your dog is quite likely to be dreaming about ... you!

DOGGIE SENSES

SUPER SMELL POWER

Dogs experience the world differently to us. We find our way through the world mostly through sight and sound, while dogs live in a world of smells and find their way by following their noses. The part of a dog's brain that is dedicated to smell is four times bigger than in humans. Dogs can sniff a patch of grass and find out all sorts of things: They can tell what dogs have passed by and when; whether they are male or female; and much more. It really is a doggie superpower!

DOGGIE VISION

Generally speaking though, dogs see less well than we do. It's an old myth that dogs see in black and white. They can see in colour, but they see less of a range of colours than us. They can see shades of yellow and blue, but can't tell the difference between red and green. Dogs can't see textures or details as well as we can, but their night vision is much better than ours – they can see things moving in the dark much better than we ever can.

Did you know? It is estimated that dogs have nearly 220 million cells in their noses to detect smell, while we have just 5 million. It is believed that they can even use this super sense to detect diseases such as cancers and diabetes.

SUPER HEARING POWER

Hearing is another doggie superpower. They can hear sounds from much further away than we can – up to four times further. They can also hear much higher frequencies or pitches than we can. The frequency range of dog's hearing is 40–60,000 Hertz, whereas the human hearing range is 20–20,000 Hertz. Some dog whistles are silent to the human ear but can be heard by dogs. Sometimes your dog can hear something coming way before you can.

MORE DOGGIE SUPERPOWERS

Dogs have some other abilities that we don't even understand. Some dogs seem to sense when their owners are coming home even before they have left school and will wait by the door. Some dogs can find their way home over huge distances – distances that would take more than a good sense of smell. They seem to possess some secret sense of direction and navigation, and they have endless determination.

Are they guided by the stars? By the Earth's magnetic field? We just don't know. Dogs have some sort of sixth sense that we don't yet understand.

Did you know? A dog's nose print is as unique in identifying them as our fingerprint is to us.

HEALTH

Your dog's health is the key to a happy and fun life for both of you! She will need a yearly health check by a vet.

HOW TO KNOW YOUR DOG IS FEELING UNWELL

If your dog's behaviour changes, it might be because she is unwell. She can't tell you what's wrong, so you will have to watch her body language and how she acts.

- Is she doing anything unusual?
- Does she seem unhappy?
- Is she eating less food than usual? Or more?
- Is she going to the toilet in the house, or in other places she shouldn't?

Doggie sense: Your dog should be vaccinated against common diseases and treated as necessary for fleas, worms and ticks.

GOING TO THE VET

Some dogs are happy to go to the vet, but others get nervous and distressed.

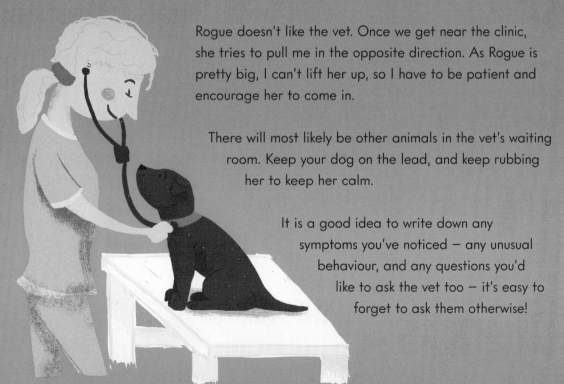

Rogue doesn't like the vet. Once we get near the clinic, she tries to pull me in the opposite direction. As Rogue is pretty big, I can't lift her up, so I have to be patient and encourage her to come in.

There will most likely be other animals in the vet's waiting room. Keep your dog on the lead, and keep rubbing her to keep her calm.

It is a good idea to write down any symptoms you've noticed — any unusual behaviour, and any questions you'd like to ask the vet too — it's easy to forget to ask them otherwise!

MICROCHIPPING

All dogs in Ireland have to be microchipped, meaning that a vet inserts a tiny electronic chip under their skin. It is so small that they don't know it's there. If your dog gets lost, whoever finds him can bring him to a vet or animal shelter where his chip can be scanned and your dog identified.

AGEING

Just like humans, dogs slow down as they get older. Older dogs sleep more, but they still need plenty of exercise — it's important that they stay active and engaged with the world through walks and play. Like people, dogs have different stages of life:

- Puppyhood: Puppies need a lot of training and attention. They must learn all about themselves and the world around them.

- Adolescence: They are not small, floppy puppies any more, but fast and energetic teenagers, intent on discovery and mischief.

- Middle age: Dogs are more settled now, happy and comfortable in their home and with their family. They have set routines and good communication with their owners.

- Elderly: Older dogs need special care to keep them comfortable and happy. They still want to explore the world every day, but they have less energy than they used to. They may walk slower and take their time to have a good long sniff.

WEATHER, SEASONS AND EVENTS

EVENTS

If there is a party or a family gathering in your house, you have to think about your dog. Where will she go? Will she be nervous with so many people? Will she get too excited and jump on younger children? It can all be tiring for a dog, so she needs a time-out area that's all her own. Have treats at the ready in case you need to entice her to a particular place or out to use the toilet, and check regularly that she's okay.

SPRING

The days are getting longer, so there is more time to walk and play! Dogs lose their winter coats in spring — they need regular brushing outside to keep their hair from taking over your home!

SUMMER

- Avoid walking your dog at the hottest times of the day — early morning and evening are better.
- Take water with you when you're out and about.
- Don't leave your dog in a car — cars can get very hot, and dogs overheat quickly. On a sunny day, your dog must have shade and cool drinking water available at all times.

Doggie sense: Thunderstorms can happen at any time of the year. The noise makes some dogs, like Rogue, very nervous. Rogue runs straight into my bed when she hears it. I let her stay there, and comfort her until the storm has passed.

AUTUMN

In the autumn, school starts again. Be sure to give your dog lots of cuddles before you leave for school and lots of attention when you return home. Even though your dog will be spending time with other members of your family, she'll be super-excited to see you when you get home.

Make sure to keep school stuff — pencils, glue sticks and so on — out of her reach, as these may be dangerous for her to chew on.

Winter is on the way, so you can let her coat grow now.

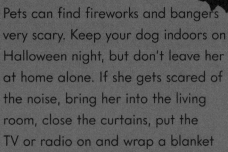

HALLOWEEN

Pets can find fireworks and bangers very scary. Keep your dog indoors on Halloween night, but don't leave her at home alone. If she gets scared of the noise, bring her into the living room, close the curtains, put the TV or radio on and wrap a blanket around her. Pet her and tell her everything is okay.

Doggie sense: Even if you think that your dog's fears are silly, they are real to her. A good owner will offer their dog comfort and safety at all times.

WINTER

Keep your dog indoors during the cold weather, and don't let her out in the garden for longer than twenty minutes at a time. If she has short hair and is quite small, you can get her a doggie jacket to wear outside.

Dogs always need a warm place to sleep. You could raise her bed off the floor in winter, using boxes or folded blankets.

With the fire blazing, it can get quite hot for a dog indoors — she may need water more than usual.

Remember, even in winter, dogs need regular walks.

WORKING DOGS AND DOG HEROES

Dogs are amazing. With their incredible senses of smell and hearing, they are real-life superheroes. There are many important and even life-saving jobs for dogs to do.

GUIDE DOGS

Labradors and golden retrievers are steady, patient and careful. This is why they make very good guide dogs. It takes many years to train a guide dog, but it is worth it — they can provide independence and freedom to visually impaired people, by guiding them across roads and around obstacles.

THERAPY DOGS

Dogs are amazing companions for the elderly, sick people and people living with different kinds of disabilities. They make people feel comfortable and offer unconditional love and friendship.

They can have a calming effect on children who feel anxious or scared.

Some charities arrange dog visits to hospitals and nursing homes. They can cheer the patients up just by being their wonderful selves. The dogs enjoy it too, because they love people and attention.

FARM DOGS

Dogs can assist farmers with various jobs, particularly herding sheep, cattle and horses. They also protect the livestock from attack by foxes, wolves and other wild animals, and act as guard dogs.

First published 2020 by The O'Brien Press Ltd,
12 Terenure Road East, Rathgar, Dublin 6, D06 HD27,
Ireland.
Tel: +353 1 4923333; Fax: +353 1 4922777
E-mail: books@obrien.ie; website: www.obrien.ie.
The O'Brien Press is a member of Publishing Ireland.

ISBN 978-1-78849-081-8

1 3 5 7 8 6 4 2
20 22 24 23 21

All of the activities in this book must be undertaken with the supervision and guidance of an adult. Young
children should not be left alone with a dog. Neither the publishers nor the author accept any legal
responsibility for the undertaking of any of the activities or exercises in this book, or for the reliance on
any advice in this book. If your dog is ill or has behavioural problems, please seek the advice of a qualified
professional such as a vet or behavioural expert.

Photo credits:
Denise Timmins-Browne: page 4 (both); Michael Corcoran: pages 5, 29, 35 (right) and inside back cover (Red, Boomer and
Minnie); Roisin Barrett: page 7 and inside back cover (Maggie); Joe Butler: pages 11, 36 and inside back cover (Scout);
Nicola Reddy: page 13 and inside back cover (Lola); Ivan O'Brien: page 19; Sharon Weldon: pages 27, 32 and 35 (left);
Susan Houlden: page 39 and inside back cover (Roxie and Missy); Bex Sheridan: page 41; Sarah Cassidy: inside back cover
(Benson); Laura Feeney: inside back cover (Molly); Megan Byrne: inside back cover (Rocky and Suki); Fionnuala McHugo:
inside back cover (Coco); Elena Browne: inside back cover (Rogue); Emma Jane Sinnott: inside back cover (Maya).

Printed and bound in Poland by Białostockie Zakłady Graficzne S.A.
The paper in this book is produced using pulp from managed forests.

Published in

DUBLIN
UNESCO
City of Literature

TAKE THE LEAD

Elena Browne
Illustrated by Jennifer Farley

THE O'BRIEN PRESS
DUBLIN